The Right Hand

of

GOD

A Psychotherapist's Case for the Reality of the Living God

Ara C. Trembly, MS, MA, LPC

ISBN 979-8-88943-403-0 (paperback)
ISBN 979-8-88943-404-7 (digital)

Christian Faith Publishing
832 Park Avenue
Meadville, PA 16335
www.christianfaithpublishing.com

Printed in the United States of America

This work is dedicated to my Lord and Savior Jesus Christ. It is also dedicated to Pastor Neil Helton, without whom this book would not exist. Finally, it is lovingly dedicated to my wonderful wife, Alison, who is a sharp editor as well as a fabulous spouse.

Introduction

"Nobody really knows what the Bible means." This was the pronouncement of a fifteen-year-old patient in my psychotherapy practice. And while I hadn't heard it so simply articulated before, this seems to be the opinion of many people: not only those who wield this statement to reject or disparage the Bible as a basis for faith but, at times, even those who struggle to make sense of God's Word to apply it to their own lives. In Bible studies and Sunday school classes across the nation and all over the world, we wrestle with the scriptures just as Jacob wrestled with God. We ponder what certain passages mean. We wonder at the motivations of the men and women portrayed. We share our own feelings and opinions about miracles recorded in the Old and New Testaments. We get entangled in debates over the possible meanings of individual words in Aramaic, Hebrew, Greek, or even English. And of course, we cite our favorite theologians as proof positive of our ideas.

But why does this have to be so difficult? If we believe the Bible is the inerrant word of an omniscient, loving, and omnipotent God, do we also think that He has created an impossibly complex theological Rubik's Cube that we need to solve in order to understand and apply that word? Surely, a God who loves us and wants us to know Him would not want to make Himself so inaccessible to those He wishes to reach. To paraphrase my brilliant wife: A loving God who makes His message clear to the world-renowned Bible scholar does the same for the poor, uneducated individual washing the floors of that scholar's office.

Of course, if we *don't* believe the Bible is the inerrant word of an omniscient, loving, and omnipotent God, we have free reign to turn the Holy Scriptures into virtually anything we wish them to be—a ticket to earthly prosperity, a hodgepodge of arcane numbers and secret codes that only the cognoscenti can interpret, or even a weapon against people and thoughts we find disagreeable or inconvenient. Books and articles that manipulate the Scriptures this way are easily found in bookstores or on the Internet, but in the work you are reading, the author fully believes that the Bible is a powerful, clear, and unambiguous message from the Creator to His creation.

Still, even the most devoted follower of the Scriptures must admit that there are differences of interpretation that can, at times, be confusing. Part of this may be because we humans simply don't think the same way that God does.

"'For My thoughts are not your thoughts, nor are your ways My ways,' declares the Lord" (**Isaiah 55:8** *New American Standard Bible*).

If we did think like God, there would only be one version of the Scriptures, and we would all fully comprehend it. But such is not the case. Some online sources state that there are as many as 233 Holy Bible translations or versions in English alone. According to *Christianity Today*:

> One of the reasons we see different versions of the Bible is because of the number of manuscripts available. There are over 5,800 Greek New Testament manuscripts known to date, along with over 10,000 Hebrew Old Testament manuscripts and over 19,000 copies in Syriac, Coptic, Latin, and Aramaic languages. ("Why Are There So Many Different Versions of the Bible?" [christianity.com])

Are there really significant differences in the overall message conveyed by these different versions and translations? In most cases, it seems the answer is no. In other cases, however, the version can make quite a difference in the way we understand what we are reading. In this book, I am leaning primarily on the New American Standard Bible (NASB) because it is widely viewed as the most literal interpretation of the Scriptures. Other versions will also be cited, however, in making points about the diversity of thought on some issues.

At this point, I must be clear about one thing. While I enjoy being a Bible teacher and a studier of the Bible, I am not a theologian. Instead, I am looking at Scripture through the lens of a psychotherapist. That means considering why an all-knowing and wise God would choose to speak to us in a way that leaves room for emotions and debate yet still arrives at the inescapable conclusion that Jesus is Lord and that God can manifest to humanity in just the right form to suit His will and the prevailing circumstances. This *does not* involve applying psychoanalysis (a questionable construct of fallen humanity) to the Almighty God who created us, which would be arrogant and absurd. It *does* mean asking some of the questions that puzzle us as flawed and sinful creatures and attempting to answer them by looking to God's Word—*and actually believing what it says*.

Chapter 1

Seeds of Debate

How many times have you sat and listened to a pastor or Christian speaker and found yourself questioning or disagreeing with something the speaker said? Truth be told, this happens often, and it is a healthy thing. In my experience, the most credible pastors and Bible teachers will always invite their listeners to check what they say against the Bible itself. But what happens when—even after we have consulted the Scriptures—we remain conflicted or unsure about an issue?

Such was the situation that sprang forth one Sunday morning when Pastor Neil Helton of Amelia Baptist Church in Amelia Island, Florida, was preaching about the book of Revelation. As I sat and mentally praised Neil for taking on such a challenging book from the pulpit, it was a chance remark that started my mind working in a different direction. Neil cited the following verses:

> *Revelation 5:1* *New American Standard Bible*
> **The Scroll with Seven Seals**
> I saw in the right hand of Him who sat on the throne a scroll written inside and on the back, sealed up with seven seals.

> *Revelation 5:7* *New American Standard Bible*
> And He came and took the scroll out of the right hand of Him who sat on the throne.

He added, almost as an aside, that since God is spirit, He doesn't actually have a right hand.

Somehow this little throwaway stopped me. Wait a minute, my therapist brain said, *Why would God mention His right hand in Holy Scripture if He in fact doesn't have one?* Answering for Neil in my mind, I thought that the reason must be that John, the human author of Revelation, is using a metaphor. One of the definitions for metaphor in *The American Heritage Dictionary* is as follows: "One thing conceived as representing another; a symbol."

As a therapist, I am constantly looking to make sense of what patients tell me to help them make sense of their lives. The idea that God (the divine author of Revelation) chose and wanted to use the phrase, "right hand," but have it represent something else just didn't seem to make sense to me in this case. The Scripture says that the scroll was *in* God's right hand and was taken *out* of God's right hand. Of course, I could guess that perhaps the Lord was using this phrase to mean the locus of His power or some other such thing. But in that case, my therapist mind asked, *Why not simply say that? Why mention his hand at all? And why His* right *hand? Why not simply say what You mean—unless what You said is what You mean?*

At that point, of course, I was no longer paying attention to the message on Revelation. Instead, I went scampering down a mental rabbit hole. There I continued to be the therapist, continuing to ask questions, continuing to try to make sense out of this issue. I thought, *Is Jesus not God? And did Jesus not have real flesh and blood hands?* Surely the Scripture confirms this. Then again, we are talking about God, the Father, here, so perhaps that's where the difference lies. Yet are we humans not "created in His image"? If that is so, why is it so difficult to conceive that God has hands that are at least somewhat similar to human hands?

After some further mental gymnastics, I stopped my inner debate and concluded that God, being omnipotent, can certainly have hands if He wants them. I decided to talk to Neil after the service. As Neil and I shook hands afterward, I mentioned my little conundrum and my conclusion that an omnipotent God could certainly manifest hands if that was His will. Neil wasn't buying it, however, and reminded me of the following statement from Jesus Himself: "God is spirit, and those who worship Him must worship in spirit and truth" (*John 4:24 New American Standard Bible*).

A spirit, as we think of spirits, is a ghost—immaterial and perhaps invisible to the human eye. It doesn't have hands per se; at least not hands that can affect material objects or people. But why not, if that spirit is the omnipotent, everlasting God? Why should we place limitations on the God through whom *all things are possible*? While it seemed we weren't going to agree on this topic, I still felt admiration for my pastor's solid biblical stance. I shook Neil's hand again and said, "God does have a right hand, and I am shaking it right now." I think that set him back for an instant, but at that moment, I just wanted Neil to know how much I appreciated him. I thought the debate over this rather whimsical idea was done. It seems the Holy Spirit had other ideas, however.

Later that evening, I got ready for bed and settled in for my usual eight hours of blissful slumber. It is important to note here that rarely do I awaken for any substantial period during the night. This night would be different. At about three in the morning, my mind awoke, or more accurately, my questioning therapist mind awoke—and it wasn't rolling over and going back to sleep. While I hadn't yet done any research, I knew that God's right hand is mentioned several times (actually some fifty-five) in Scripture. Why would the Lord repeatedly use this phrase if it wasn't accurate? One of the rules I had been taught about biblical exegesis is that if something in Scripture is mentioned more than once, it is likely very important. And even if there is a metaphorical meaning to this important phrase, why could it not be both factual *and* metaphorical? For that matter, just what does being "made in God's image" actually mean if not that in some ways we resemble God?

These and many more questions rolled over and over in my mind. I tried to tell myself that this wasn't a life-and-death issue and that I needed some sleep. Still, the debate continued more vigorously than ever. At some point, I prayed that the Lord would let me put this question aside and go to sleep. Almost immediately came the answer. This was an important idea, and I needed to research these questions and record the results in a book. Realizing that, I promised myself and the Lord that I would follow up on this manner, and I felt completely relieved. I slept peacefully the rest of that night, and in the following days, the research began in earnest.

Chapter 2

God's Appearance

Reality. What a concept!

—Robin Williams

What exactly does the God of the Bible look like? Certainly, this is a question that has crossed all of our minds at some time. I have yet to see any consensus image, although Scripture is replete with descriptive data. An Internet search on the question reveals scores of images, many of them clearly depicting visual speculations on Jesus but relatively few claiming to represent God the Father. Those images that are described as Father God are almost always powerful and stern looking, often from classical paintings. In these images, God has long gray or white hair as well as a full white beard. Shimmering light, white clouds, or lightning are also frequently seen. In some pictures, He bears a striking resemblance to Charlton Heston in *The Ten Commandments*.

Yet we do have a visual description of God—the Ancient of Days—in the following passage:

> I kept looking
> Until thrones were set up,
> And the Ancient of Days took *His* seat;
> His garment *was* white as snow,

And the hair of His head like pure wool.
His throne *was* ablaze with flames,
Its wheels *were* a burning fire. (***Daniel 7:9***
New American Standard Bible, The Ancient of
Days Reigns)

From this description we see that God has a vivid, white garment (which presumably covers a body) and that He has a head with hair. The description of God's hair says it is "like pure wool," which implies a certain texture based on our experience with wool. Thus, we have a description that goes beyond the mere visual to an impression we experience through our sense of touch. As a result, we have a fuller idea of God's physical reality in this situation. We should also remember that pure wool is unadulterated and of the finest quality, altogether fitting for the Creator of the universe.

Finally, we see that the Ancient of Days sits on a blazing throne with wheels—not something we would picture a spirit doing but certainly something that a being with a human form could do. Perhaps this is merely a physical manifestation of the Spirit that is God, but it begs the question as to why the Lord would manifest in what appears to be human form. There is no mention of the face, however, and this makes sense. Scripture tells us that if God were to show Himself to us, we mere mortals would not survive the experience if we were to look upon His face. He says as much to Moses in the following passage: "He further said, 'You cannot see My face, for mankind shall not see Me and live!'" (***Exodus 33:20*** *New American Standard Bible*).

But if we believe this, what do we make of the following verse? "So Jacob named the place Peniel, for *he said*, 'I have seen God face to face, yet my life has been spared'" (***Genesis 32:30*** *New American Standard Bible*).

To answer this, let us consider the fact that Jacob's wrestling match took place at night and ended just as the dawn was breaking. It seems unlikely that in the dark, Jacob got a clear look at the face of the "man" with whom he struggled. It is highly doubtful that Jacob could later pick this "man" out of a police lineup. So if he did indeed see God's face, he didn't see it very clearly.

Further, the "man" does not identify himself when Jacob asks him who he is, instead asking Jacob, "Why is it that you ask my name?" As a psychotherapist, it is relatively common for me to do something similar in talking with patients. For example, suppose a patient tells me that his life has been falling apart ever since he began an extramarital affair then asks me, "What should I do?" When the answer is obvious, my response to this will often be something like, "Why are you asking a question to which you already know the answer?" (The answer, of course, is that he should immediately end the affair.) Similarly, Jacob undoubtedly had an idea with whom he was wrestling because he later states it outright.

We will look further into this question later.

Meanwhile, what can we logically infer from all of this? One key point is that Scripture tells us that God does have a face as well as some other humanlike characteristics. And if He has these aspects of human form, why should we disbelieve that He has hands?

As noted previously, in the New American Standard Bible, the right hand of God (or the Lord, Most High, Majesty, etc.) is referred to some fifty-five times, not counting references to Jesus' right hand. The references come in both the Old and New Testaments with an amazing twenty-four references in Psalms alone. The phrase "hand of God" appears fifteen times with some overlap. I have been unable to find any reference to God's left hand.

The mentions of God's right hand often come in the context of His exercise of divine creative power.

> Assuredly My hand founded the earth,
> And **My right hand** spread out the heavens;
> When I call to them, they stand together. (*Isaiah 48:13* *New American Standard Bible*)

Sometimes, we are also told that more than the divine hand is involved.

> The Lord has sworn by **His right hand and by His mighty arm**:

"I will never again give your grain *as* food
for your enemies,
Nor will foreigners drink your new wine
for which you have labored." (***Isaiah 62:8*** *New
American Standard Bible*)

These are not the only biblical references that describe, or at least hint at, the body parts of our Almighty God, but for the moment, let's stick with our discussion of His powerful right hand.

Chapter 3

The Right Stuff

We might well ask why God's right hand is mentioned so much and the left hand never. According to WebMD, "Right-handed people dominate the world, and it's been that way since the Stone Age. How do we know? Researchers figured it out by measuring the arm bones in ancient skeletons and by examining wear patterns in prehistoric tools. In Western countries, lefties make up only about 10 percent of the population. Folks who favor different hands for different tasks (mixed handed) or who use both hands with equal skill (ambidextrous) are uncommon" ("Differences Between Left- and Right-Handedness" [webmd.com]).

The right hand is dominant in most of humanity, and with that goes the idea that it is the stronger hand, the hand through which one's "power" is likely to be asserted. A right-handed boxer, for instance, is likely to deliver his most powerful punches with his dominant right hand. Thus, the wielding of power and creative force via God's right hand makes sense in terms of the way most humans are built and in terms of the way we understand such things. We are, after all, created in His image. But more on that later.

It is also useful to consider the various meanings of the term "right." We use this word to denote something that is correct, as in, "I got nine out of ten answers right on the quiz." This also extends to ideas we deem to be morally correct, as in, "There's never a wrong time to do the right thing." For believers, everything our God does is right, that is to say, morally correct. The use of our Creator's right hand, however, emphasizes not only the infinite power of the Lord but also the idea that He commits His full strength to the carrying out of His perfect will.

According to *Merriam-Webster*, "right" also means suitable or appropriate. This touches on the familiar idea of "using the right tool for the job." It's difficult to imagine, for example, that most of us would use a sledgehammer to hang a picture on our living room walls. God's choice of tools is similarly suitable, even if it isn't always clear at first. Not only is the tool "right," but the effort exerted with the tool is always "just right." To be sure, the Lord has used what most of us would consider some very unlikely "tools" or methods—or people—to accomplish His divine purposes. Consider how even a prostitute was lionized in Scripture because she was used by God to carry out His plan when she sheltered the spies sent out to Jericho by Joshua (see Joshua, Chapter 2).

> ***Hebrews 11:31*** *New American Standard Bible*:
> By faith **the prostitute Rahab** did not perish along with those who were disobedient, after she had welcomed the spies in peace. [bolding mine]

> ***James 2:25*** *New American Standard Bible*
> In the same way, was **Rahab the prostitute** not justified by works also when she received the messengers and sent them out by another way? [bolding mine]

Consider also that this prostitute has the distinct honor of being part of the direct bloodline that led to Jesus.

> Ram fathered Amminadab, Amminadab fathered Nahshon, and Nahshon fathered Salmon. Salmon fathered Boaz **by Rahab**, Boaz fathered Obed by Ruth, and Obed fathered Jesse. Jesse

> fathered David the king… Jacob fathered Joseph
> the husband of Mary, by whom Jesus was born,
> who is called the Messiah. (bold mine) (*Matthew
> 1:4–6, 16 New American Standard Bible*)

*****

In the world of mental health, we may casually refer to someone who is mentally ill as not being in their "right mind." Here the term "right" refers to what most of us would call "normal," but it also could mean "healthy," as in, "After my bout with the flu, I'm feeling all right today."

Merriam-Webster also offers "genuine" and "real" as alternate definitions of our term, and such adjectives would certainly apply to the thoughts and actions of Almighty God. In fact, if we consider "real" and "true" to be synonyms (and many of us do), we get a broader sense of what Jesus is saying in the following passage: "Jesus said to him, 'I am the way, and **the truth**, and the life; no one comes to the Father except through Me'" [bolding mine] (*John 14:6 New American Standard Bible*).

In the most complete sense, Jesus (thus God) is Himself the definition of reality and truth. This idea is extremely difficult for many to accept because it means that we as humans are not the creators of "our" truth and "our" reality. While it is popular today to speak in such terms, these are mere fantasies. Some psychologists might call this "wish fulfillment." It is the fashion in our culture to tell everyone that whatever they believe is true and real is, in fact, objectively true and real, even if others might find it absurd or offensive. The culture also considers it rude and cruel to disabuse anyone of his or her own unique truth and reality. But even a casual look around us confirms that we have not created reality and we are not in control of it, and this is a frightening notion to many. Being in control of one's life makes one feel safe and secure. But being subject to the control of an "outside" reality may seem anxiety provoking.

The idea that every individual creates his or her own reality and morality obviously flies in the face of our experience, yet like most sinful thoughts, it is very appealing. This is the same notion that Satan expounded to Eve in the Garden of Eden when he told her that eating from the tree of the knowledge of good and evil would enable her to "become like God, knowing good and evil" (Genesis 3:5). If one is indeed "like God" (omnipotent, omniscient), it follows that there is no need for God or for the rules He has laid down in His law or for the reality He has created and in which we live. Denial of objective reality is the means by which we can shake our collective fist at the God who created us and build our lives around the sinful ideas and behaviors we choose.

Those of us who counsel patients often see denial at work in the minds and hearts of patients who simply cannot bear to face some uncomfortable reality in their lives. This is often referred to as a defense mechanism because believing it defends the individual against the anxiety and discomfort that may come with facing objective reality. Our job as healers, however, is not to support and encourage this fanciful strategy but instead to speak the truth in love and help our patients deal with what is objectively real.

A culture that rejects God in favor of some self-created reality allows virtually any kind of sin to be redefined as an "acceptable" individual preference. This fits perfectly with any individual's self-centered moral code—and is therefore labeled by the culture as valid. Anything that challenges that individual code must not even be entertained because it would presumably harm the individual's fragile self-esteem. Thus, we now see mind-bending ideas trumpeted despite their conflict with objective reality. A person born male (a biological reality) can now "identify" (redefine) himself as a female—*just by saying so*—and the rest of us are somehow obligated to accept this. Suddenly we must begin addressing this person with female pronouns and allowing "her" to compete in women's athletics despite the obvious advantages "her" male hormones provide. In some cases, we are even required to pay, through our taxes, for gender-changing hormones and surgeries. But as Sigmund Freud is reputed to have said, "Biology is destiny."

When we ignore objective reality, there is no longer a standard for right and wrong. In that case, virtually anything can be called "right," at least by cultural standards. Yet the obvious truth is that the *culture* has *not* created the universe and all that is in it, including human beings. The reality of God as Creator is all around us. This is why it is especially important to realize that everything about God's truth **is right in every sense of that word**. Having created everything our senses can perceive, as well as what cannot be perceived, He literally has "the whole world in His hands." Fortunately for mankind, He is a loving God who doesn't want anyone to perish spiritually—that is, to suffer punishment that includes eternal separation from Him. Thus, there is no need for invented versions of reality to make us feel better about ourselves.

Yet another use of the term "right" is found in hillbilly and old West vernacular. If someone is described as "right smart," our term may mean "very" or even "supremely." This makes perfect sense since for the believer, God is supreme in His every aspect.

Then there is the usage in which "right" denotes something acceptable or preferable as when we say, "She knows all the right people." In Scripture especially, sitting at God's right hand is considered something that is not only correct but incredibly favorable. In several passages, Jesus, once He departs from earth and returns to heaven, is described as sitting in the place of highest honor at the right hand of God.

> ***Mark 16:19*** *New Living Translation*
> When the Lord Jesus had finished talking with them, he was taken up into heaven and sat down in the **place of honor at God's right hand.**
> [bolding mine]

> ***Luke 22:68–70*** *New American Standard Bible*
> And if I ask a question, you will not answer. But from now on the Son of Man will be seated at the **right hand of the power of God.**" And they all said, "So You are the Son of God?"
> And He said to them, "You say *correctly* that I am." [bolding mine]

With this last passage, we may be tempted to say that Scripture does indeed use God's right hand to refer to His almighty power, and I certainly wouldn't argue with that. But if the passage refers *only* to God's power and not a physical right hand, I am having trouble visualizing just *what* Jesus sat down next to. If Jesus is sitting next to a spirit, which has no physical form, how do we even know where the right side of that spirit is located? If we then say that perhaps God the Father is a phantom or shade that appears to have physical form (but does not), are we now saying that Jesus sat down at the right hand of a ghost or an illusion? It just doesn't make sense.

In the book of Acts, Luke, who often furnishes readers with more detail that his fellow Gospel authors, emphasizes not only God's hand but His ownership of same. Thus, Jesus doesn't just sit to the right of something that *looks* like a hand but next to the hand that *belongs* to God the Father.

"God exalted him to his **own** right hand as Prince and Savior that he might bring Israel to repentance and forgive their sins" [bolding and emphasis mine] (**Acts 5:31** *New International Version*).

Adding a bit of physical reality to the idea of God's sitting, we also have a place to be seated.

> ***Hebrews 12:2*** *New American Standard Bible*
> Looking only at Jesus, the originator and perfecter of the faith, who for the joy set before Him endured the cross, despising the shame, and has sat down **at the right hand of the throne of God**. [bolding and underline mine]

> ***Hebrews 12:2*** *New Living Translation*
> We do this by keeping our eyes on Jesus, the champion who initiates and perfects our faith. Because of the joy awaiting him, he endured the cross, disregarding its shame. Now he is seated in the place of honor **beside** God's throne. [bolding mine]

Hebrews 12:2 *Young's Literal Translation*
Looking to the author and perfecter of faith—Jesus, who, over-against the joy set before him—did endure a cross, shame having despised, on the **right hand** also of the throne of God **did sit down**. [bolding mine]

All this certainly suggests a physical location. And the only way to make sense of that location is to point to the objective reality of God's throne and His almighty right hand.

Chapter 4

In His Image

As mentioned previously, some passages in Scripture have been and continue to be debated among Bible scholars and among the many who simply want to understand the truth of God's Word. High on the list of such passages is the following:

> Then God said, "Let Us make mankind **in Our image**, according to **Our likeness**; and let them rule over the fish of the sea and over the birds of the sky and over the livestock and over all the earth, and over every crawling thing that crawls on the earth." So God created man **in His own image**, in the **image of God** He created him; male and female He created them. [bolding mine] (**Genesis 1:26–27** *New American Standard Bible*)

Let us first consider the idea that God the Father is fundamentally spirit as Scripture clearly says. This is absolutely true, but if He is *limited* to being spirit, much of the Bible is now rendered difficult to understand. If we as humans are created in God's image and God is *only* spirit (without physical dimensions, without molecular structure, invisible, without shape and size, ghostly, etc.), then how does that translate to the reality of our own physical bodies, which do indeed have physical dimensions, molecular structure, shape, size, and visibility? Does a spirit even have an image? If so, what does that image appear to be? Clearly, we humans don't fit most accepted definitions of spirit in visual terms. Thus, at least in the earthly realm, we are not created in *that* image.

As one might expect, much is made of the exact meanings of the words "image" and "likeness" (in Hebrew, "*tselem*" and "*demut*"), which are used in some versions of the text we are considering.

Some sources maintain that the words "image" and "likeness" are defined identically. They take these passages as metaphorical, insisting that being made in God's image refers to our potential as created beings to understand and relate to our Creator. We are beings with a mind and a soul, set apart from mere animals. These scholars suggest that being made in God's image means that, clearly in a limited way, we are like God mentally, creatures with the capacity for thought. We have the ability to form ideas, to reason, to create on a limited scale, and to make choices—including moral choices.

It is obvious that we are like our Creator in these ways, but does the passage in question preclude the idea that our physical appearance may also resemble God's? I believe there are no wasted words in Scripture, so if our Lord mentions both "image" and "likeness," they must each have their own meanings and nuances. God never explains exactly how we resemble his "image," but at least some scholars point out that this word in the Septuagint is the same word used to describe a "copy" of an original. Similarly, "likeness" may describe an actual image (as in "That painting is a good likeness of him.") or points of agreement other than visual (as in "He thinks just like his dad."). This would allow us to conclude that humans bear some physical resemblance to our Creator (hands, face, perhaps more), as well as likeness on a mental, emotional, and even behavioral level (anger, for example, is an emotion shared by God and humans).

> Then God said, "Let us make humanity in
> our image **to resemble us** so that they may take
> charge of the fish of the sea, the birds in the sky,

the livestock, all the earth, and all the crawling things on earth."

God created humanity in God's own image, in the divine image God created them, male and female God created them. [bolding mine] (***Genesis 1:26–28*** *Common English Bible*)

Some variations in opinions are seen below:

***Christianity Today*:**

Theologians debate whether humans being made in God's image (Genesis 1:27) has a physical component. It is possible there is a God-given design to why humans look the way they do, and perhaps our physical design (our limitations, our abilities) tells us something about how we are God's image bearers. ("Do We Know What God Looks Like? What the Bible Says" [christianity. com])

Image definition and meaning—Bible Dictionary (biblestudytools.com):

Some have referred *"image"* to man's bodily form and *"likeness"* to his spiritual nature (Justin Martyr, Irenaeus). **That it connotes physical resemblance to God. It may be admitted that there is a secondary reference to the Divine dignity of the human body; but this does not touch the essence of the matter, inasmuch as God is *not represented as having physical form*.** [italics mine]

Since we have already seen that Scripture tells us that God has hands and a face, I would argue that God the Father is most certainly represented at times as having a physical form, and we will examine those passages in the chapters to come.

Chapter 5

Is God Physical?

The appearance of God, who is spirit, in some physical form is called a theophany. According to BibleStudyTools.com, a theophany is defined as "manifestation of God that is tangible to the human senses. In its most restrictive sense, it is a visible appearance of God in the Old Testament period often, but not always, in human form." One of the more obvious and well-known of God's manifestations is seen in the passages concerning the burning bush. Of course, there is no human form involved here, but there is an appearance of God that involves fire, which is a gas and is thus physical.

> ***Exodus 3:2–6*** *New American Standard Bible*
> **The Burning Bush**
> Now Moses was pasturing the flock of his father-in-law Jethro, the priest of Midian; and he led the flock to the west side of the wilderness and came to Horeb, the mountain of God. Then the angel of the Lord appeared to him in a blazing fire from the midst of a bush; and he looked, and behold, the bush was burning with fire, yet the bush was not being consumed.
>
> So Moses said, "I must turn aside and see this marvelous sight, why the bush is not burning up!"

> When the Lord saw that he turned aside to look, God called to him from the midst of the bush and said, "Moses, Moses!" And he said, "Here I am." Then He said, "Do not come near here; remove your sandals from your feet, for the place on which you are standing is holy ground." And He said, "I am the God of your father—the God of Abraham, the God of Isaac, and the God of Jacob."
>
> Then Moses hid his face for he was afraid to look at God.

When Moses decides to investigate an unusual phenomenon, we are first told that "the angel of the Lord" appears to him in the fire of a bush that burns but is not consumed. Who is the angel of the Lord? There appears to be quite a bit of debate about this. It is also interesting to note that although the angel "appeared," we are not given any description of his appearance unless we take the fire itself to be the angel's appearance. If we stopped reading this passage at verse 3, we would logically assume that an angelic being had manifested to Moses in the midst of a blazing fire in the bush. But then it is the Lord who sees Moses turning to look and God who calls to Moses from the midst of the bush.

Many scholars assume that this "Lord" and "God" is the same being who previously appeared in the bush, yet the inescapable fact that the text now calls Him Lord seems to say otherwise. Angels would never be referred to as "Lord." The text does not say, "Then the angel called to Moses…" It does say that *God* called to Moses. When we consider this, it makes much more sense to say that perhaps an angel got Moses' attention, then the Lord Himself spoke to Moses of the mission which he would later accomplish.

In GotQuestions.org ("Who is the angel of the Lord?"), we are told:

> The precise identity of the "angel of the Lord" is not given in the Bible. However, there are

> many important "clues" to his identity. There are
> Old and New Testament references to "angels of
> the Lord," "*an* angel of the Lord," and '*the* angel
> of the Lord.' It **seems** when the definite article
> "the" is used, it is specifying a unique being sepa-
> rate from the other angels. The angel of the Lord
> speaks as God, identifies Himself with God, and
> exercises the responsibilities of God. (bold mine)

Without a precise biblical definition, the authors are left to express what "seems" to them to be the truth. This is a strategy we see often among commentators when the exact meaning of a biblical term or passage is unclear, and it is certainly useful. An educated guess may be valuable. Nevertheless, we must not confuse an opinion—even a well-informed opinion—with verified fact. While some believe that *this* angel is actually God Himself, that seems (there's that word again!) to conflict with the idea that angels are, in fact, *created* by God for the purpose of serving Him, often as a messenger. Instead, the text indicates that there is an angelic appearance followed by a theophany.

Whichever view one takes of the angel of the Lord, however, it is clear that in this passage God does appear in a form that is physical and is observable via the human senses. It is perfectly reasonable to conclude that the burning bush existed in physical reality. That physical reality claims to be God. We are not told that Moses saw some fiery image or hallucination, but there are some today who actually believe that.

An Israeli professor of cognitive philosophy claims in a 2008 journal article that the burning bush was a "drug-induced hallucination." According to the professor, two naturally existing plants in the Sinai Peninsula have the same psychoactive components as ones found in the Amazon jungle and are well-known for their mind-altering capabilities. The drugs are usually combined in a drink known in the Americas as ayahuasca ("Moses Was High on Drugs, Israeli Researcher Says"—*ABC News* [go.com]). Nowhere are we told, however, that the ancient Israelites were partaking of this psychotropic cocktail. And the idea that the ingredients were at hand is hardly proof that the drink was made or consumed. Some Internet sources say that evidence of ayahuasca use dates back one thousand years based on archaeological findings in Bolivia. Neither the timeline nor the geographical location of the biblical account, however, suggest that it would have been in use when Exodus was written between 1440 and 1400 BC.

But since we are considering the resemblance of human beings to their Creator, let us move on to focus on God's more "humanlike" appearances in Scripture.

Chapter 6

Jacob, the Wrestler

The story of Jacob wrestling with God is certainly one that may invite psychological interpretation, especially since it involves powerful emotions and a reported physical encounter—a wrestling match—with God, who is essentially a spirit. This episode could be seen as a true encounter with God, as a dream, as a psychic manifestation of Jacob's internal struggles, or simply as an impromptu wrestling match with some unknown person who might be an angel.

First let us consider Jacob's mental and emotional state. It is worth noting that Jacob's history where his twin brother Esau is concerned is one of conflict and deception. In fact, Jacob's name literally means "supplanter" or "someone or something taking the place of another, as through force, scheming, strategy, or the like" (Dictionary.com). Jacob was born holding his twin brother's heel, and his name may also be interpreted as "holder of the heel." As the twins (not identical) grew, they could not have been more different from each other. Jacob seems to have been a quiet man who stayed home in the family tents a lot and was his mother's favorite. Esau, on the other hand, was a rough-and-tumble individual who is described as "a skillful hunter, a man of the field." Esau was their father's favorite.

The struggle between the twins actually began while they were still in the womb.

Genesis 25:21–23 *New American Standard Bible*

Isaac prayed to the Lord on behalf of his wife, because she was unable to have children; and the Lord answered him, and his wife Rebekah conceived. But the children struggled together within her; and she said, "If it is so, why am I *in* this *condition*?" So she went to inquire of the Lord.

And the Lord said to her,

"Two nations are in your womb;

And two peoples will be separated from your body;

And one people will be stronger than the other;

And the older will serve the younger."

Jacob later induces the apparently naïve Esau into giving up his birthright (as the oldest son) for a bowl of lentil stew that Jacob was cooking. When the time comes for Isaac to bestow his traditional blessing on his sons, Jacob and his mother Rebekah scheme to deceive old and blind Isaac into blessing Jacob in Esau's place. This includes a web of lies told by Jacob to his dying father. When Esau finds out about the chicanery, he asks his father to bless him as well, but Isaac tells him that the blessing had already been given and that Jacob has already been named as Esau's "master." This must have been especially galling for Esau as the older brother and presumed inheritor of the bulk of his father's estate. Esau then vows to kill Jacob. Rebekah, hearing this, sends Jacob away to live with her brother Laban.

It is with this history between the brothers that we are brought to the time of Jacob's encounter. In a chapter which the New

American Standard Bible entitles "Jacob's Fear of Esau," we see the following:

> ***Genesis 32:9–11*** *New American Standard Bible*
>
> Then Jacob said, "God of my father Abraham and God of my father Isaac, Lord, who said to me, 'Return to your country and to your relatives, and I will make you prosper,' I am unworthy of all the favor and of all the faithfulness, which You have shown to Your servant; for with *only* my staff I crossed this Jordan, and now I have become two companies. Save me, please, from the hand of my brother, from the hand of Esau; for I fear him, that he will come and attack me *and* the mothers with the children.

Jacob realizes he is obviously unworthy before God, but he must also realize that he is unworthy because of his sin: the well-documented lies, scheming, and deception toward his twin brother. It is not unreasonable to assume that Jacob feels guilty for his sins against his brother. He may even believe that he deserves to die at Esau's hand after he treated Esau so badly. It is also possible that Jacob is trying to somehow justify the scheming actions of his own mother, who he presumably loves. The fact that he fears someone who has openly threatened to kill him seems obvious, but the situation is complicated by Jacob's realization that Esau might well be justified in taking revenge. This fear is heightened by the news from Jacob's messenger that Esau is approaching with four hundred men at his side. Jacob then divides his entourage into two groups so that if one group is killed, the other might survive.

These conflicting feelings likely put Jacob into a state of extreme stress and moral uncertainty. Not only is Jacob's own life in danger, but his scheming and trickery have now put the lives of his family and the entire entourage in danger. It would be no surprise if Jacob was feeling completely overwhelmed by what he feared might happen, as well as by his own culpability. Perhaps he is experiencing what psychologists call "cognitive dissonance," defined by *Merriam-Webster* as "psychological conflict resulting from incongruous beliefs and attitudes held simultaneously."

Perhaps more to our point, one source (https://www.medical-newstoday.com/articles/326738) says of cognitive dissonance that "It refers to the mental conflict that occurs when a person's behaviors and beliefs do not align." If we assume that Jacob has been raised to respect and practice God's law, it is obvious that his behavior toward Esau does not reflect these beliefs. The same source cited above notes that "As people generally have an innate desire to avoid this discomfort, cognitive dissonance has a significant effect on a person's behaviors, thoughts, decisions, beliefs and attitudes, and mental health. People experiencing cognitive dissonance may notice that they feel anxious, guilty, and ashamed."

All this certainly describes Jacob's mental, emotional, and spiritual predicament. Jacob then sends his two wives and children away, fearful of the carnage to come. This is the kind of situation that keeps one up at night worrying. Now comes the struggle.

Jacob Wrestles

Then Jacob was left alone, and a man wrestled with him until daybreak. When *the man* saw that he had not prevailed against him, he touched the socket of Jacob's hip; and the socket of Jacob's hip was dislocated while he wrestled with him.

Then he said, "Let me go, for the dawn is breaking."

But he said, "I will not let you go unless you bless me." So he said to him, "What is your name?"

And he said, "Jacob."

Then he said, "Your name shall no longer be Jacob but Israel; for you have contended with God and with men and have prevailed."

And Jacob asked him and said, "Please tell me your name."

But he said, "Why is it that you ask my name?" And he blessed him there.

So Jacob named the place Peniel, for *he said,* "I have seen God face to face, yet my life has been spared."

Now the sun rose upon him just as he crossed over Penuel, and he was limping on his hip. Therefore, to this day the sons of Israel do not eat the tendon of the hip, which is on the socket of the hip, because he touched the socket of Jacob's hip in the tendon of the hip. (**Genesis 32:24–32** *New American Standard Bible*)

Who is this "man" with whom Jacob wrestles? The answer depends on how we view this event. If this is a dream, a psychological interpretation might hold that the "man" is some aspect of Jacob's own psyche. This makes perfect sense in light of the cognitive dissonance struggle described above. Perhaps this is the very picture of the conflict between a man's cherished beliefs and his sinful nature, which may act in opposition to those beliefs. Even if this event is not a dream, it could certainly be a psychic manifestation of Jacob's internal struggle.

Some have sought to portray the "man" as an angel sent to bring Jacob to a realization about himself. Other sources claim this is the guardian angel of Esau. Yet the text does not seem to support the idea that this is any kind of angel.

Many believe that Jacob is wrestling with God Himself. This seems to be what Jacob later believed. Then again, it is difficult to think that any mortal could prevail in hand-to-hand combat with the Creator of the universe. It is also unlikely that Jacob could have held his own against an angel since those beings clearly have strength and powers superior to humans. We can reasonably conclude, however, that Jacob is struggling with God if we remember that our Lord can take whatever form pleases Him to bring about His purposes.

Again, if viewed from a psychological perspective, we can state with some certainty that Jacob must have had an internalized belief in

God's nature and moral character. If we then say that Jacob is struggling against the nature and character of God—which would have forbidden Jacob's treachery—it makes sense to say that he is contesting with God. God could certainly have manifested as a wrestler far mightier than Jacob, but that would not have allowed the Lord to have this wonderful teaching moment. Instead, the Almighty in the form of a "man" allows the wrestling match to continue all night. The victory is easily achieved by a mere touch that dislocates Jacob's hip. This could obviously have been done at the start of the struggle, but the struggle is the point of the lesson. This symbolizes the battle every one of us has against thoughts and actions that run contrary to God's character. God's character has won. Jacob clearly sees this as he now holds on to the "man" and requires a blessing. An ordinary man could certainly never have supplied a life-changing blessing, nor would he have had any authority to change Jacob's name to Israel— more evidence that this manifestation is God the Father.

As mentioned previously, Jacob knew full well with whom he had wrestled. But what are we to make of the remark that he had seen God face-to-face? In addition to the points mentioned previously, it is useful to note here that the word "face" does not exclusively describe a person's physical countenance. In defining the term, *Merriam-Webster* cites an "archaic" notion that "face" could also refer to one's *presence*. The year 1400 BC certainly qualifies as archaic. It also seems logical to assume that if he had seen the Lord's physical countenance and survived, Jacob would certainly have described that countenance just as Daniel did.

But Scripture does not describe Jacob wrestling with the Ancient of Days as chronicled in Daniel. On this occasion, He chose to appear in a different form that could directly engage Jacob and reshape his very conscience. We can deduce from the circumstances that Jacob certainly did come face-to-face with the person of God; and he can truly say that having come face-to-face with God, he survived. God in His mercy showed *that* face to Jacob and not only allowed him to live but to prosper.

This experience also spells the end of Jacob's cognitive dissonance along with the beginning of God's blessings toward Jacob.

When Esau finally catches up with Jacob, the feared brother is overjoyed to see Jacob again and seems to hold no grudge. Jacob, who once grabbed for whatever he could seize, is now generous in bestowing gifts on his brother.

> Then Esau ran to meet him and embraced him, and fell on his neck and kissed him, and they wept.
>
> He raised his eyes and saw the women and the children and said, "Who are these with you?"
>
> So he said, "The children whom God has graciously given your servant."
>
> Then the slave women came forward with their children, and they bowed down. And Leah likewise came forward with her children, and they bowed down; and afterward Joseph came forward with Rachel, and they bowed down.
>
> And he said, "What do you mean by all this company which I have met?"
>
> And he said, "To find favor in the sight of my lord."
>
> But Esau said, "I have plenty, my brother; let what you have be your own."
>
> Jacob said, "No, please, if now I have found favor in your sight, then accept my gift from my hand, for I see your face as one sees the face of God, and you have received me favorably. Please accept my gift which has been brought to you, because God has dealt graciously with me and because I have plenty." So he urged him, and he accepted *it.* (**Genesis 33:4–11** *New American Standard Bible*)

Note that in verse 10, Jacob tells Esau, "For I see your face as one sees the face of God." Clearly, Jacob is not saying that Esau looks like God. Instead, Jacob is describing the look on his brother's face as one that reflects the presence of the Lord. This fits nicely with Matthew Henry's recitation of the text below in his Bible Commentary (1704):

> And Jacob said, "Nay, I pray thee, if now I have found grace in thy sight, then receive my present at my hand: for therefore I have seen thy face, *as though* I had seen the face of God, and thou wast pleased with me." [Italics mine]

God has done a wonderful teaching and healing work in these brothers, and He has done it through a theophany that fit the situation perfectly. This is a fine example of our God's love for us and of His complete understanding of our spiritual and emotional needs.

Chapter 7

A God of Many Parts

Lest we should believe that the preceding examples of God's physical manifestations are mere hallucinations or perhaps an attempt by the human authors of Scripture to wax poetical, let us consider some additional scriptures.

First we will look at the familiar story of Shadrach, Meshach, and Abed-nego, who were thrown into a blazing-hot furnace as punishment for not bowing down and worshipping the golden image of Babylonian King Nebuchadnezzar. Such an action would clearly have violated the Jewish commandment regarding idol worship.

> Then Nebuchadnezzar in rage and anger gave orders to bring Shadrach, Meshach, and Abed-nego; then these men were brought before the king.
>
> Nebuchadnezzar began speaking and said to them, "Is it true, Shadrach, Meshach, and Abed-nego, that you do not serve my gods, nor worship the golden statue that I have set up? Now if you are ready, at the moment you hear the sound of the horn, flute, lyre, trigon, psaltery and bagpipe, and all kinds of musical instruments, to fall down and worship the statue that I have made, *very well*. But if you do not worship, you will imme-

diately be thrown into the midst of a furnace of blazing fire; and what god is there who can rescue you from my hands?"

Shadrach, Meshach, and Abed-nego replied to the king, "Nebuchadnezzar, we are not in need of an answer to give you concerning this matter. If it be *so*, our God whom we serve is able to rescue us from the furnace of blazing fire; and He will rescue us from your hand, O king. But *even* if *He does* not, let it be known to you, O king, that we are not going to serve your gods nor worship the golden statue that you have set up."

Daniel's Friends Protected

Then Nebuchadnezzar was filled with wrath, and his facial expression was changed toward Shadrach, Meshach, and Abed-nego. He answered by giving orders to heat the furnace seven times more than it was usually heated. And he ordered certain valiant warriors who *were* in his army to tie up Shadrach, Meshach, and Abed-nego in order to throw *them* into the furnace of blazing fire. Then these men were tied up in their trousers, their coats, their caps, and their *other* clothes and were thrown into the middle of the furnace of blazing fire. For this reason, because the king's command *was* harsh and the furnace had been made extremely hot, the flame of the fire killed those men who took up Shadrach, Meshach, and Abed-nego. But these three men, Shadrach, Meshach, and Abed-nego, fell into the middle of the furnace of blazing fire *still* tied up.

Then Nebuchadnezzar the king was astounded and stood up quickly; he said to his counselors, "Was it not three men *that* we threw bound into the middle of the fire?"

They replied to the king, "Absolutely, O king."

He responded, "Look! I see four men untied *and* walking about in the middle of the fire unharmed, and the appearance of the fourth is like a son of *the* gods!"

(***Daniel 3:13–25*** *New American Standard Bible*)

The obvious conundrum is the identity of the fourth man who appears like "a son of the gods." Just what does "a son of the gods" look like? And which gods is Nebuchadnezzar referring to? According to one source (https://www.chabad.org/library/article_cdo/aid/4451665/jewish/Nebuchadnezzar.htm), Nebuchadnezzar "bowed to the sun and other idols," but he did not deny the existence of the Jewish God. Since Nebuchadnezzar refers to the plural "gods," however, it makes more sense to believe that he was referring to the Babylonian gods. According to one source (https://symbolsage.com/babylonian-gods-a-list/), while there were many Babylonian gods and goddesses, "Marduk is considered to be the primary deity of Babylonia and one of the most central figures in the Mesopotamian religion. Marduk was considered to be the national god of Babylonia and was often simply called 'Lord.'" Marduk did have at least one son, Nabu, who is described by Wikipedia as follows: "Nabu wore a horned cap and stood with his hands clasped in the ancient gesture of priesthood. He rode on a winged dragon known as Sirrush that originally belonged to his father Marduk."

Unfortunately, this doesn't seem to be the individual the text is describing, which leaves us with little idea of what kind of "man" the king is seeing. Perhaps Nebuchadnezzar is simply at a loss for words in trying to say just what kind of man this is.

In verse 28 of this same chapter, however, Nebuchadnezzar exclaims: "Blessed be the God of Shadrach, Meshach, and Abednego, who has sent His angel and rescued His servants who put their trust in Him" (Dan. 3:28 NASB). Although he describes the fourth man as God's "angel," at this point, Nebuchadnezzar leaves no doubt that "God" is the God of Shadrach, Meshach, and Abed-nego.

This identification is further complicated by differences in biblical interpretation as seen in other translations of verse 25.

"He answered and said, 'Lo, I see four men loose, walking in the midst of the fire, and they have no hurt; and the form of the fourth is like *the Son of God*" [italics mine] (***Daniel 3:25*** *21st Century King James Version*).

This translation would support the view of some that this manifestation was a preincarnate appearance of Christ, especially given the capitalization of "Son" and the use of the article "the," rather than "a." Other translations, however, give a different view.

"But he exclaimed, 'Look! I see four men, not tied up, walking around there in the flames, unhurt; and the fourth looks like one of the gods'" (***Daniel 3:25*** *Complete Jewish Bible*).

This translation is notable because it does not use the word "son," and it refers to multiple gods, which would be more in line with the king's presumed theology. Some may suggest that because this version by a Messianic Jewish Bible scholar is striving to reach a Jewish audience, any mention of a "son" would be avoided to eliminate the possibility that this is the Son of God. But the following translation by another Messianic Jewish scholar would argue against that:

"He answered and said, 'Lo, I see *anashim arba'ah* (four men) free (not bound, loose), walking in the midst of the *eish* (fire), and they have no hurt; and the form of the fourth is like the *Bar Elohin* (Ben Elohim, Hebrew)" [italics mine] (***Daniel 3:25*** *Orthodox Jewish Bible*).

According to one source (https://www.bibliatodo.cobm/en/bible-dictionary/bar-elohin), one of the definitions of "*Bar Elohin*" is "Son of God." Similarly, another source, Hebrew Interlinear Bible (OT), translates the phrase as "like the Son of God."

I confess that, as a Christian, I would love to be confident that this is the preincarnate Christ, but one thing troubles me about this idea. How would Nebuchadnezzar or anyone living at that time have any idea what "the Son of God" would look like? Obviously, no one in that age had seen Jesus, so we can discount the idea that He was recognized in the furnace. It seems much more likely that Nebuchadnezzar and the others who witnessed this miraculous event were dazed, confused, and simply at a loss to describe the individual in question—a "man" who could withstand impossibly hot temperatures and apparently extend that capability to those with him. This fruitless search for adequate words might well explain the description changing from "Son of God" to God's "angel."

Clearly, our understanding of this passage is going to be significantly influenced by the translation we read. If we believe the fourth figure in the furnace is God in some form, including Christ, we must also believe this was a theophany. But we would also find support if we insisted that this was an angel since Nebuchadnezzar himself eventually came to that conclusion. If the multiple different translations leave us wondering, however, we must say we just don't know who or what was in that fire with the three others. This is a perfectly acceptable answer, and for many of us, it is an honest one.

The fact that the translations agree that this fourth individual was in the form of a "man," however, tells us that if this was God in the furnace, He chose to take that form. This should not be surprising given that we see this in many places in Scripture.

Now above the expanse that was over their heads, there was something resembling a throne, like lapis lazuli in appearance; and on that which resembled a throne, high up, *was* **a figure with the appearance of a man.** Then I noticed from the appearance of His waist and upward *something* like gleaming metal that looked like fire all around within it, and from the appearance **of His waist** and downward I saw something like fire; and *there was* a radiance around Him. Like the appearance of the rainbow in the clouds on a rainy day, so *was* the appearance of the surrounding radiance. **Such *was* the appearance of the likeness of the glory of the Lord.** And

> when I saw *it*, I fell on my face and heard a voice
> speaking. [bolding mine] (***Ezekiel 1:26-28*** *New
> American Standard Bible*)

Here we see a figure that appears to be a man. He has a waist and is seated, just as a human being might be, on a throne. The New American Standard Bible 1995 refers to His "loins" rather than His waist. In either case, this is said to be a description of the glory of the Lord. Some commentators might assume that since God is spirit, we must explain His appearance in human form. But why is any explanation necessary? Why should the Almighty need a footnote to explain His choice to appear in this fashion? Even more to the point, why would we humans require such an explanation of Him? Are we so arrogant that we cannot allow for the absolute power and absolute wisdom of God to express itself in the way that our God prefers? When we insist that God, being comprised of spirit, cannot have physical humanlike form, we in essence declare that His power is limited. Thus, when Scripture tells us that He does in fact show Himself in human form, we turn theological backflips trying to explain this. Consider the following from Matthew Henry in reference to these passages in Ezekiel:

> *This was the glory of the Lord,* in which he was pleased to manifest himself a glorious being; yet it is not *the glory of the Lord,* but *the likeness of that glory,* some faint resemblance of it; nor is it any adequate likeness of that glory, but only *the appearance of that likeness,* a shadow of it, and not the very *image of the thing.*

Henry says that this *was* the glory of the Lord, yet it was *not* the glory of the Lord. Perhaps this is a likeness with a "faint resemblance" to the actual glory, but it is not even an adequate likeness. This is just a "shadow" of the likeness and definitely not the very image of the thing. This is rather like saying this is a copy of a copy of a copy of a document rendered multiple times over (we keep recopying each copy) on a copier with outdated technology to the point where it bears little resemblance to the original document. These are the lengths some will go to to deny the power of God to manifest physically or otherwise through the human senses as a humanlike figure.

Perhaps we could dismiss this incident as a simple hallucination or as a divine appearance that nevertheless has no basis in physical reality. But the prophet also hears the voice of God giving him detailed instructions. Is this now both a visual and auditory hallucination? That might be the explanation offered by those who do not believe in the living God, but for those with faith, this is certainly not a figment of Ezekiel's imagination.

Finally, we come to a theophany witnessed by many individuals, a theophany in which God's resemblance to human form is again emphasized.

> Then Moses went up with Aaron, Nadab and Abihu, and seventy of the elders of Israel, **and they saw the God of Israel**; and **under His feet** there appeared to be a pavement of sapphire, as clear as the sky itself. Yet He did not reach out with **His hand** against the nobles of the sons of Israel; and they saw God, and they ate and drank. [bolding mine] (***Exodus 24:9–11*** *New American Standard Bible*)

All those who went with Moses up the mountain were privileged to have seen God without being destroyed. God chose not to "reach out" His powerful hand to kill those who beheld His glory. We are given no reason for this extension of privilege by our God, yet it seems from what we know of the reverence the Jews held for the Almighty that these individuals dared not look at His face. It wouldn't surprise us to learn that they refused to gaze any higher than His feet! Yet there *were* feet, and they were standing on some sort of jewellike pavement. It seems logical that if the observers had glimpsed the fullness of God's physical glory, they would have fully described such a wonder. We don't think of invisible spirits as standing, nor do we particularly describe them as having feet. God's physical reality is unquestionable, however, even if the observers chose not to look at or describe all of His reality.

> Then Moses, Aaron, Nadab, and Abihu, and seventy of the elders of Israel went up [the mountainside], and they saw [**a manifestation of**] the God of Israel; and under His feet there appeared to be a pavement of sapphire, just as clear as the sky itself. Yet He did not stretch out His hand against the nobles of the Israelites; and they saw [**the manifestation of the presence of**] God and ate and drank. [bolding mine] (***Exodus 24:9–11*** *Amplified Bible*)

The amplified translation above seeks to explain God's reported physical appearance, as well as the survival of the observers in the presence of the glory of God, by inserting brackets in order to call what happened a "manifestation." Presumably, this phrasing implies that this appearance of God is something less than a simple physical fact. When we seek to define the term "manifestation," however, we find several interesting results. One *Merriam-Webster* definition is "a perceptible, outward, or visible expression" of something. It seems this is what the Amplified Bible is driving at. If this is a mere "visible expression" of something, it could also be said not to have any physical reality, thus it might also be called a spirit or even a hallucination.

Another *Merriam-Webster* definition of manifestation is "an occult phenomenon, specifically: materialization." Of course, if something is materialized, it has *material* qualities such as physical reality that can be perceived by human senses. On the other hand, spirits are also described as materializing.

Merriam-Webster offers a plethora of synonyms for manifestation, including abstract, avatar, embodiment, epitome, icon, image, and incarnation. Some of these provide for a physical reality (embodiment, incarnation) while others (abstract, avatar, image) seem to deny such a reality. Inserting this type of phrasing in translating is a convenient way of sidestepping the issue of God's physical reality in these passages, but we really shouldn't have to *add* anything to a passage to clarify its meaning. The translations are near unanimous in agreement that these people "saw the God of Israel."

And now we know that God the Father also has feet and that He stands on those feet—a decidedly human thing to do. This is one affirmation of the truth that we are indeed created in His image.

Chapter 8

Psychotherapy and God

At this point, some readers may be wondering why this author has chosen to apply some concepts drawn from psychotherapy to our understanding of Holy Scripture and to the nature of God. The truth is that psychotherapy sheds some light on the way we humans think, although not nearly as much light as Scripture itself. Psychotherapy has nothing to add to the Word of God, but it can help illuminate the ways we interpret that Word, or the reasons we might want to try and bend the meaning of the Word to suit our own purposes. It may also, as in the case of Jacob, help explain why some characters in Scripture behaved the way they did.

According to the American Psychological Association, "psychotherapy involves communication between patients and therapists that is intended to help people:

- Find relief from emotional distress as in becoming less anxious, fearful, or depressed
- Seek solutions to problems in their lives, such as dealing with disappointment, grief, family issues, and job or career dissatisfaction
- Modify ways of thinking and acting that are preventing them from working productively and enjoying personal relationships."

Readers may also be aware that there are many theories of psychotherapy, so we cannot point to any one theory and call that psychotherapy. In fact, according to www.cbtcognitivebehavioraltherapy.com, there are at least four hundred different theories in psychotherapy. Many of those theories, however, do have much in common, including the key role of "unconscious" desires and motivations. In the interest of transparency, my comments on psychotherapy derive primarily from the psychodynamic view. This view is "a form of talk therapy that explores the connection between a patient's past experiences—often from childhood—and their current mindset. Psychodynamics describes the psychological and emotional forces that interact in a person's mind" (https://www.psychology.org/resources/what-is-psychodynamic-therapy/).

When individuals seek out counseling, whether from a Christian practitioner or a non-Christian, they do so because they feel angry, depressed, disappointed, anxious, or otherwise disturbed in their daily lives. While they will furnish many reasons for their feelings, what they actually want can often be summed up in a single word: peace. Consider Odysseus, hero of ancient mythology, who after an adventurous life of near-death challenges and ultimately triumphs, chose near the end of his life to live quietly and happily with his wife for many years. It is said that he survived to a ripe old age and died peacefully. This kind of idyllic peace—whether or not our earthly lives are lengthy—is perhaps a limited preview of what is offered to believers in Christ.

Broadly speaking, however, I have found that psychotherapists as a "community" have much difficulty with any belief in God. To be sure, some psychotherapists are proclaimed believers, but most, in my experience, will avoid bringing God or any spiritual beliefs into the counseling office. Unless they are educated in a Christian setting, God will have had no place in their training. There is sometimes a nonspecific nod to "spirituality" by some who acknowledge that spiritual beliefs may be a valuable aspect of the person and of the healing to take place, but that is as far as it goes.

In his essay, "Of God and Psychotherapy," *American Journal of Psychotherapy* (psychiatryonline.org), T. Byram Karasu, MD, asserts:

> Those who have recovered from their **primitive innocence** need to formulate their ideas of God and religion, regardless of their affiliation with a religious community. One may need to resonate emotionally with the God of his or her religion but intellectually need to transcend all its dogma and cultivate a personal concept of divinity **free from any theological structure**. Such an **enlightened person** achieves enduring equanimity by striving to own the attributes of Gods—to be godly. This is equally true for psychotherapists as it is for their patients. [bold mine]

Here we are told that we need to recover from what Karasu calls our "primitive innocence" to formulate ideas of God and religion. Yet childlike innocence, which is unspoiled by the corruption of the world, is the very way we *must* approach our ideas of God. As Jesus Himself puts it in the following passage:

> Now they were bringing even their babies to Him so that He would touch them; but when the disciples saw *it*, they *began* rebuking them.
> But Jesus called for the little ones, saying, "Allow the children to come to Me, and do not forbid them, for the kingdom of God belongs to such as these. Truly I say to you, *whoever does not receive the kingdom of God like a child will not enter it at all.*" [italics mine] (***Luke 18:15–17** New American Standard Bible*)

Karasu also tells us that to believe in God and to practice religion, all of us need to intellectually transcend the dogma of our religious teachings and cultivate our own personal concept of divinity "free from any theological structure." I find this is highly representative of the messages and mindset I see in today's psychotherapeutic community. Intellect is their idol and their God while religion and spirituality are viewed as the provinces of the primitive and uneducated masses.

One suspects that many in our modern psychotherapeutic community would agree with Karl Marx in the following quotation:

> Religious distress is at the same time the expression of real distress and the protest against real distress. Religion is the sigh of the oppressed creature, the heart of a heartless world, just as it is the spirit of a spiritless situation. It is the opium of the people. The abolition of religion as the illusory happiness of the people is required for their real happiness. The demand to give up the illusion about its condition is the demand to give up a condition which needs illusions. (*Critique of Hegel's Philosophy of Right*)

The key to Karasu's earlier quotation is that we are encouraged to *cultivate our own personal concept* of divinity, thus our own version of the truth. Once we do this, we as individuals become the arbiters of truth and the creators of reality, seemingly fulfilling Satan's promise to Eve in the Garden of Eden: "You will become like God, knowing good and evil" (Genesis 3:5). This is delusional thinking at its worst, although it certainly aids the evil cause of mankind's enemy, the devil. Karasu then doubles down on this delusion when he asserts that once we break free from the shackles of religion and create our own reality, we are in fact "enlightened." We now *own* "the attributes of Gods" (note the plural Gods). We are by definition "godly" because we have assumed His throne.

According to Karasu:

> The attributes of religion and God are separate but highly intertwined. Attributes of reli-

gion pull us down to earth, and their purpose is to civilize humanity. Attributes of God pull us up to the heavens, and their purpose is to make humans godly. In tandem they make us soulful and spiritual beings, and they provide meaning to our lives. These grounding predicates of God and religion also offer a remedy for the common cognitive dissonance between organized religion and our need to be true to ourselves.

It is important to remember that the attributes of religion and God spoken of here are those created by each individual for himself or herself. Karasu claims that it is these attributes as we understand them that actually create "gods." "Attributes that serve the divine needs define God, for example, compassion is God. It is not that God is love but rather that love is God; it is not God is mercy, but it is mercy is God; it is not God is truth, but the truth is God. In short, the attributes of God are Gods themselves," he says. Thus it might be possible to have eight billion or so different versions of these attributes worldwide—eight billion Gods!—because *universal* truth that applies to every created creature is a concept that is unacceptable to many psychotherapists.

Further, it is laughable to say that there is cognitive dissonance between organized religion and our need to be true to ourselves, implying that the latter is much more important. In reality, it is our own sinful nature that often determines whether or not we define something as "true to ourselves." The Bible reminds us that our "true selves"—our hearts, if you will—are basically wicked.

> The heart is more deceitful than all else
> And is desperately sick;
> Who can understand it? (*Jeremiah 17:9*
> *New American Standard Bible*)

When a mass murderer declares that he has done his horrible deeds to be true to himself, do we accept this as an excuse and allow him to go free? Even in today's Godless world, we would certainly not do that. Yet the society *will* excuse nearly every kind of sin, debauchery, and even the destructive acts of rioters in the name of people being "true" to themselves.

This is the very battle that Jacob fought in his wrestling match with God, and it is the battle that we all face as residents of a fallen world. As psychotherapists, it is our task to steer patients away from delusion (for instance, the belief that you can create your own reality, morality, and truth) and toward the truth that there is only one reality—the one created by God. And that reality is the same for every one of us, mammoth efforts of denial notwithstanding. Having a firm grasp on reality is one way in which we can truly be counted as acting in concert with the infinite power that rests in the mighty Right Hand of God.

Chapter 9

Omnipotent and Omniscient

Up to this point, we have been focusing on the omnipotence, or unlimited power, of God. We have also seen evidence that we are indeed created in His image, both emotionally and physically. While we fully agree that God is fundamentally spirit, we also fully agree that He can become matter in any form and at His will—an idea that may be foreign to mankind's version of physics but not to metaphysics. According to *Merriam-Webster*, "Just as *physics* deals with the laws that govern the physical world (such as those of gravity or the properties of waves), metaphysics describes what is beyond physics—the nature and origin of reality itself, the immortal soul, and the existence of a supreme being."

Whenever we attempt to put limits on God's power, we are essentially doubting His omnipotence. This is the kind of thinking that goes into creating so-called superheroes of fiction, individuals who have incredible powers "far beyond those of mortal men" but who are regularly challenged and nearly defeated. Or perhaps the superhero has a weakness others can exploit as when the indestructible "man of steel" is brought low by a substance (kryptonite) that comes from his home planet. Characterizing such heroes as mighty, yet vulnerable, makes for fascinating story lines because they are clearly <u>not</u> omnipotent. It follows that a superhero who really *was* *all-powerful* would always win every battle, thus making for very predictable stories. Yet this idea exemplifies the very clear meaning of the word "omnipotent." According to *Merriam-Webster*, "Although *omnipotent* is most often used in general contexts to mean 'having virtually unlimited authority or influence' (as in 'an omnipotent war-lord'), its original applications in English referred specifically to the power held by an almighty God."

Thus, to assert that an all-powerful God could take only one form would be to deny that He has the power to take other forms. But it is never wise to sell God short when it comes to His almighty power.

Yet another way in which we fall into the trap of limiting God's power is to deny that He is omniscient, that is, all-knowing. To be sure, God sometimes will ask questions of us, but we should never make the mistake of believing He doesn't know the answers. If our young child, for example, swipes some unauthorized cookies from the cookie jar, and we witness the deed, we might still ask the question, "Who took those cookies out of the jar?" We are not asking because we don't know. We are asking because we want to elicit a certain response from our child—in this case, a confession of guilt, hopefully followed by repentance. This is a moral teaching moment. Consider the following exchange between God and Adam and Eve:

> Then the Lord God called to the man, and said to him, "Where are you?"
>
> He said, "I heard the sound of You in the garden, and I was afraid because I was naked; so I hid myself."
>
> And He said, "Who told you that you were naked? Have you eaten from the tree from which I commanded you not to eat?"
>
> The man said, "The woman whom You gave *to be* with me, she gave me some of *the fruit of* the tree, and I ate."
>
> Then the Lord God said to the woman, "What is this *that* you have done?"
>
> And the woman said, "The serpent deceived me, and I ate." (**Genesis 3:9–13** New American Standard Bible)

Are we to believe that an almighty and all-knowing God did not know where Adam was? Of course not. Like any loving parent, God is asking the question for a purpose. As in the case of our cookie-stealing child, the purpose is to elicit a confession of guilt. And like a child, Adam seeks to change the subject, asserting that he hid from God because he was naked—something that had apparently never bothered him before. When God calls Adam on this bit of distraction, he seeks to shift the blame to Eve, who gave him the fruit of the forbidden tree. In fact, by calling her "the woman whom You gave *to be* with me," Adam is actually trying to blame God, Himself, for starting all this trouble by providing him with a mate. Eve, for her part, says she was deceived by the serpent, so she ate the forbidden fruit. These again are common tactics used by children and adults who try to squirm out of culpability in difficult situations.

Next, we have God, in His earthly form as Jesus, asking a question:

> And a woman who had suffered a *chronic* flow of blood for twelve years, and could not be healed by anyone, came up behind Him and touched the fringe of His cloak, and immediately her bleeding stopped.
>
> And Jesus said, "Who is the one who touched Me?"
>
> And while they were all denying it, Peter said, "Master, the people are crowding and pressing in on You."
>
> But Jesus said, "Someone did touch Me, for I was aware that power had left Me."
>
> Now when the woman saw that she had not escaped notice, she came trembling and fell down before Him, and admitted in the presence of all the people the reason why she had touched Him, and how she had been immediately healed.
>
> And He said to her, "Daughter, your faith has made you well; go in peace." (*Luke 8:43–48* New American Standard Bible)

As the earthly embodiment of the omnipotent and all-knowing God, Jesus knows full well who has touched Him. In this case, however, He doesn't seem to be saying that she did anything wrong. Rather, His purpose in asking who had touched Him was to deliver another wonderful teaching moment, primarily for His disciples and those in the crowd—and for us as readers of Scripture.

Jesus' disciples were ready to forget the matter since the crowd was milling around in close proximity to them, and it was likely that more than one had incidentally touched Jesus. But it is worth noting that these incidental touches were just that—accidents. The touch of the afflicted woman, however, was far from accidental. It was purposeful and was done for a singular reason. And it was driven by faith. In this case, the word "touch" may also encompass the idea of "reaching out to."

The disciples didn't see the point of singling out one person. They didn't realize that a miraculous healing had occurred, but Jesus insisted the healed one identify herself—not so that He could criticize or embarrass the woman or gain accolades for Himself but so that God's glory might be manifest in this significant moment.

When the woman did come forward, she told her story, allowing all at the scene to hear about what a great healing had taken place. Jesus did not criticize her for having the temerity to touch "the fringe of his cloak." Instead, our Lord praised her for her faith and gave credit to that faith for her healing. Besides the woman herself, Jesus was probably the only person who did know the answer to His question. By making what was conceived as a "secret" healing into a public event, Jesus gave glory to God and taught all around Him about the importance of faith. Such teaching remains essential and powerful to this day.

Chapter 10

Doing Our Part

Thus far, we have spent much time and thought asserting the physical reality and the ineffable omnipotence and omniscience of Almighty God. That's because these ideas are critical to understanding the incomparable entity with whom we are dealing when we invoke His name, and particularly when we study His word. God is real, in both the physical and spiritual sense. He is not just a nice idea dreamed up by ancient scribes who had nothing better to do than to create a supreme being. He is not a lifeless idol or statue sitting in a temple. He is not a psychological construct fashioned to confirm someone's theory of the mind. He is the Creator and the embodiment of both the physical and metaphysical realities. The idea that He is fundamentally spirit doesn't change the fact that when He chooses to be, He is also fundamentally physical.

We have described some of the efforts over centuries to make the Lord somehow less mighty—somehow less knowing—so that we might be able to control Him to some degree, to create our own version of him, or at least to slip by somewhere on a Biblical technicality—thus having things our own way. Unfortunately for those who wish to dither with the Word, this strategy won't work with a being who is the very definition of perfection.

> ***Matthew 5:47–48*** New American Standard Bible
> And if you greet only your brothers *and sisters*, what more are you doing *than others*? Even the Gentiles, do they not do the same? Therefore you shall be perfect, *as your heavenly Father is perfect.* [last italics mine]

> ***Deuteronomy 32:4*** New American Standard Bible
> The Rock! His work is *perfect,*
> For all His ways are just;
> A God of faithfulness and without injustice,
> Righteous and just is He. [italics mine]

> ***2 Samuel 22:31*** New King James Version
> *As for* God, His way *is perfect*;
> The word of the Lord *is* proven;
> He *is* a shield to all who trust in Him. [italics mine]

> ***Psalm 19:7*** New American Standard Bible
> The Law of the Lord is *perfect,* restoring the soul;
> The testimony of the Lord is sure, making wise the simple. [italics mine]

When we come right down to it, God is perfect, and we are not. God's Word is also perfect. Yet many of us want to think of ourselves as "basically good people" who obey "most" of what is prescribed in Scripture. And because we try so hard to be "basically good," we want to believe that God will take us home to be with Him in heaven at the end of our earthly days. As reported in 2020 by *Christian News* (https://christiannews.net/2020/06/26/survey-shows-most-americans-believe-humans-are-basically-good-but-dont-think-life-is-sacred/), a survey by Dr. George Barna found that most Americans (69 percent) believe that human beings are "basically good." But the Bible insists that we acknowledge the reality that, far from being "good," we have hearts that are wicked and sinful by God's perfect standard. Logically, if all it takes to get to heaven is that we be "basically good" by the world's standards, those of us who think of ourselves as "basically good" would assume we are heaven bound no matter what God thinks of the state of our lives and our behaviors. But God is all-seeing and all-knowing, and there is a reason we need to constantly ask Him for forgiveness of our sins.

"But the Lord said to Samuel, 'Do not look at his appearance or at the height of his stature, because I have rejected him; for God does not *see* as man sees, since man looks at the outward appearance, *but the Lord looks at the heart*'" [italics mine] (*1 Samuel 16:7* New American Standard Bible).

We must then face the reality that from birth, we are creatures with sinful hearts which are only too well known to our Creator. Since this is the case, we might wonder why a holy God would pay any attention to us, much less actually love us enough to sacrifice his own Son—the very Creator of the universe—so that we might be pardoned from our sins and allowed to live with Jesus throughout eternity.

> What is man that You are mindful of him,
> And the son of man that You visit him?
> For You have made him a little lower than the
> angels,
> And You have crowned him with glory and
> honor.
> You have made him to have dominion over
> the works of Your hands;
> You have put all *things* under his feet,
> All sheep and oxen—
> Even the beasts of the field,
> The birds of the air,
> And the fish of the sea
> That pass through the paths of the seas.
> (*Psalm 8:4–8* New King James Version)

Why does God love us? Why has He even gone so far as to honor us as described in the above passage? It certainly can't be because we are deserving of such love and honor. The truth is many of us have spent much of our lives running away from Him because we knew we couldn't meet His perfect standard on our own merits. We know our own wicked thoughts; we remember our harmful actions, and we remember our willful turning away from God to a path we knew was wrong. So fully knowing who we are and what we have done, why does a perfect God love us anyway? The answer is seen in the following passage:

God Is Love

Beloved, let's love one another; for love is from God, and everyone who loves has been born of God and knows God. The one who does not love does not know God, because **God is love**. By this the love of God was revealed in us, that God has sent His only Son into the world so that we may live through Him. [bolding mine] (*1 John 4:7–9* New American Standard Bible)

God loves us because it is His very nature. God *is* love. He doesn't love us because we have done marvelous works in His name or because we have said wonderful things about Him. He clearly doesn't love us because we have any kind of hold over Him. But love is a choice, and He has actually *chosen* to love us. This is a hard concept for us to grasp because most of us will not choose to love someone we view as wicked and sinful. But unlike a human, God sees everything about us—not just our physical, moral, and emotional warts and wrinkles but our shining potential as well. It is that potential that allows us to be used by God as instruments in His mighty right hand, just as Moses, Samson, Rahab, and countless other unlikely souls have been used to fulfill His divine purposes.

How then can we see this manifesting in our own lives? Certainly, we can pray and ask God to bring us opportunities every day to serve His kingdom. We can also ask Him to make us more aware when such opportunities arise and to give us the wisdom, strength, and courage to follow through by acting on those opportunities. It is not unusual for such opportunities to take us out of our comfort zones, but God never promised the heroes of the Bible that they would be comfortable. Anxiety is the enemy, and it is fully enabled by our spiritual enemies. On our own, we may feel scared and incapable of doing what God asks. God, however, brings peace and courage to our hearts if we will only seek His face, hear His voice, and commit to serving Him.

In his fascinating book, *Becoming Elijah*, author and scholar Daniel C. Matt tells a Hasidic tale in which a pious Jew asked his rabbi why the prophet Elijah never appeared on the night of the Seder even though the door was left open for him, and the customary goblet of wine was waiting on the table. The Rabbi told him, "There is a very poor family in your neighborhood. Go visit them and propose that next year you and your family will celebrate Passover with them in their house and that you will provide everything they need for the whole holiday. Then on the night of the Seder, Elijah will certainly come." The man did as he was told, but after the following Passover, he returned to the rabbi, complaining that once again Elijah had failed to appear. The rabbi responded, "Elijah came but you couldn't see him." Holding a mirror to the man's face, he continued, "Look, this was Elijah's face that night."

Could you be Elijah, or Moses, or Samson to someone in your life, even somebody you don't know? Could you be the unlikely instrument that is wielded by God's mighty right hand to comfort that person, or to bring healing, or to inspire hope? Our God has a plan for each of us, and He intends to carry it out regardless of whether or not we cooperate. But we *can* make the decision to cooperate by seeking God's will for us. All it takes is a willingness to follow God's leading and a heart that embraces the infinite and unstoppable power and wisdom of the living God.

I encourage you to be in prayer about this daily and to look for opportunities to be a blessing as the Lord directs. And when God calls your name, may your enthusiastic response be, "Here I am, Lord! May I be led and strengthened by Your mighty right hand!"

About the Author

Ara C. Trembly, MS, MA, LPC. His background includes graduate study in psychology at New York University and Rutgers. He holds a master's degree in counseling from Philadelphia Biblical University and a master's degree in communication from Fairleigh Dickinson University. Mr. Trembly is a licensed professional counselor in the State of Georgia and is a board-certified hypnotherapist (International Hypnosis Federation). He is also a Christian counselor (member, American Association of Christian Counselors), writer, consultant, and highly experienced public speaker. Mr. Trembly was also a faculty member of Philadelphia Biblical University's (now Cairn University) Institute of Higher Learning.